Honeymoon Shoes

Honeymoon Shoes

First Printing: 2023

ISBN: 978-1-952869-84-6

Cover Art by Valyntina Grenier
Design, Editing & Layout by C. M. Tollefson
Cathexis Northwest Press

cathexisnorthwestpress.com

Honeymoon Shoes

Poetry by Valyntina Grenier

Cathexis Northwest Press

for Jane

Table of Contents

Is There One Chance for This Leaden Verse	1
To Lovers Who Canoe the Day	2
Square Dance	3
City's Limit	4
Frailer Neighbors	6
Deities and the Human Brain	7
Score Sustenance	8
Dress Our Souls	9
Petal	15
You're Mine You	17
Pressed Against This Smart Glass	18
Ololyga	20
Beginning and End	24
Papas/ Dead on the Ground	25
My Scapegoat Wound	27
This You an Echo November Abandons	28
Under Trees	29
Sources	30
About the Hype	31
An Oh Well Star	32
About the Type	49
Rub a Raw Slice Down the Middle or Modern Plants	50
Valediction Forbidding Treason	51
Taking the Lady's Hand and Passing Her Back Her Bag	52
Transparent Kitchen	53
Little One/ What Love	54
Left Hand It the World Rolling	55
Ecologue	56

Is There One Chance for This Leaden Verse

Among the shadows of these pillars
I draw each capitol's ruined shape

a plump heart donned w/ a crown
the curve of your cheek

the gesture in your eyes
The sun hides our shadows

I lift your forefingers
to my forehead

I kiss
your wrist

I gesture and follow
under trees

I pull out a needle
and a spool of thread

to sew the straps across your slippers
while you sleep

To Lovers Who Canoe the Day

I keep coming back to the sense of floating
downriver alongside seeds
Seeds that sleeping *new something*
knew how we stand between us to disappear

the plants we seem lost to
evolutions airy need to be *just in case*
Engineering nomenclature would probably disagree
it's war on wildness We judge wickedness

judgment does bespeak feeling the necessity
of sweetest wilderness to value multiplicity lost
in centuries our destinies' rivers long for natural history's twin den
We'd be wise to save gems

the implantable useless miraculous new code/ seed
I plan once to swallow to shrink
life look— how fiercely *one for many*
the new leaf marks Grafters grift

monocultural lists of engineers They do it to shrink
evolution's possibilities say, future open/
assembly of life/ quintillions of us teeming
Biodiversity storms genes

The world created us—
holds steady *risks* this
multiplicity Risks stringing along
though good god

the crazy archive that summer afternoon
the Ohio in view
our planet in nature
eccentric by day conveyed the way

we ripped up the way
we woke the canoe to hang our weight
in seeds we balanced laughing
Each helping keep each other on the river

where the metaphor imagines a different story
for lovers of nature/ the distance/ the crew
we might see entwined again
unassailed by always together

Square Dance

No other over you for the climate fire to end this whorl in wonder desire w/ our life's great fortune confounded by virus/ police violence Cancel the rockets Spread out the world-weary sheet again over our brains/ banners/ bones Nirvana wins our hearts twin the hypotenuse to a new song on the radio we in wonder will we go with our lucky love north to Portland to the Oregon coast/ sunset sky/ halcyon line/ quiet/ freedom from heat wave of Chaos feast

City's Limit

to the memory of George Floyd

Wade out with the uprising before long police
will come with canisters of gas *kill the lights* glass shatters
Maybe too much mayhem w/ looting at a few sites
Family businesses burning

We make disasters
Storms and droughts remind me how
imperfect human power whose pristine rose really is a freak more powerful than
  corruption/ copulation/ Covid is

Capitalism atomizes
plants/ police/ rhetoric/ white supremacists kill
  people
their perfect geometry
savagely lynched

Proof of true evil
A single still image of
one wracked too scarred person too ruined to withstand fury and
  disregard
Racism governs power

my silence
white privilege
White fear
our forty-fifth president who cares

for his own mortality tweets
desires gun-toting-fake-confidence on parade
to be photographed flanked
by armed men

Karens threaten/ feel threatened/ report
a bump in a superstore or
birdwatching in Central Park
People see nature's peaceful stirring as a riot of spring cities

love off-rhythm
free green air
our new centuries-old loam
People found a garden before plagues

before rampancy/ pharmacies before enslaved
people cleared and sewed
OK legions of poets chant a word

Experience femeral nature make her way with our before-power feeling

Talk the opposite of dubious
beholding labor and intelligence
our mortal earth
the same Niagara or Everest impulse with which farmers rose-stitched Versailles

Excite/ fill us
with a sense of our equanimous power
a kind location
both literal and moral

a violent-word-wilderness
Wildness bristles w/ ambiguity and sure power
The farmer and the gardener understand power
affection on lock beyond suspension of disbelief

Protest
Harvest/ raze/ torch
the garden
Plant again

Frailer Neighbors

There's spring and grasp
spraying grass
love rolling back
two wheels on my way
home with who I was
in the garden going on
point to harvest with
late summer abundance
keeps its own garden
I simply entrail
neighbors choked and tangling
clipping some semblance of the haul
to lift off every season till frost
the moist future genes
ripen opportunity exploiting one another
trade foragers fending the sun
lividity avidly lifting destinies from their plants

Deities and the Human Brain

forgotten burgers/ lost theatre tickets our least fortunes
last laugh to dis to leap a human genus/ genius
wittingly advancing life too devoted to semper *fie*

equality never *never grant it* had Diana ocean
or pursuit in a hydroponic closet exactly heaven broke free
halcyon still like some kind of broccoli party

pushing scientists to garden wildness Consciousness
doesn't take the desire between give-in-and-take-out
the dialectical intoxicating survival of plants Plants

can alter consciousness resting our brain in a sense
like us leaning our head against the doorway of our love
Every plucked petal cast for the plants' *we might*

reinvent drives Whatever word-world desire has dance/
revolutionary actors/ all us bees pollinating equality
leaning like us between our brain and deities

Score Sustenance

There is always already a war going on

all our dead
all our little deaths

A lead heart exposed
as a chaff of grain packed in flesh

In the wake of two atomic blasts
an unknown number of hearts were made ash

The almost instantaneous expansion of
violence as air

Mortals projectile
Waves incinerate

Here we are from a page
hanging in air

Have you heard
bombs going off

Shells scatter

In a spray of shrapnel
flesh becomes mist

Bones give off carbon 13

While for you

for me
our breath becomes mist
for all
for each one

gather

Dress Our Souls

Many unsure prisoners are held silent
Caged children wail
against our alien-making laws

The guards' sadistic lives
are painted as
un-planned knowledge

A desperate don't
Stop
behind their gaze

Many gentle protestors sway
they stay
to sing a lullaby

Children fight sleep
under the guards' eyes chanting
Mamá

Many women dress our souls so
we flatten capitalism before more

mortals disappear as so many bills
flying against ourselves over eons of tools

Symbols media run are awakening
to open fields of wonder

Women w/ our arrows
before cleared plots of grass

Grave sights floor alien peace

So, posts you're running

many violent postings
out their symbol
air their impotent heart
reveal all "lovers" covered
Ignite your fears

Resign/ quit/ condemned

Only harken for many arrows

Alien peace embraces our atheism w/ poems

We bow our awakening
Our unanswering law
is running hate w/ full coverage
Knowledge faked is dim

Time's up
Let's square up
all touch all
beaten bridges

You, all betting on your laurels
shoving your tongue in your cheek
you harken
your remonstrance
we reject as lies

And you all, resting on your haunches
lawmakers laid bare
lying under your god

all violence
we eject on sight

Inside exactly one second
step off the scale

Impossible-to-thrive-with-paper-rakes
don't throw the case Don't acquit

Mend

All prisoners without cause alien your gavel

We aren't all unsure prisoners

Unsure alien— all lovers
Unsure alien— all knowing
Unsure alien— all gentle

You from a gavel held up by law war-like band you harken

all evil isn't clothed so the circle of laws mounts the peace

Petal

Rivals make haste I hear
Give good honest soldier
Belief is an apparition

Come sit down awhile
westward beating one peace
Speak to it with wonder

It would be spoken to
and will not answer fantasy
True king to thyself jump

this dead martial watch
Our state toils the subject/
the land brazen for

implements of war
whose sore task
divides the laborer

the day The whisper
goes as you know
to combat Our known

world as a sealed compact
ratified by law Life/ lands
seized against inheritance

Now mettle hot and full
in skirts list lawless
food/ enterprise/ our state

Strong hand take it
the main motive/ the source/
the chief head comes armèd

The mind's eye in little graves
the sheeted dead
as stars/ trains of fire/

disasters/ the sun
Influence stands
sick to doomsday

Eclipse fear/ fate/ omens
Earth, blast me
The cock crows

Stay and speak
Don't strike Stand
Tis' here we do wrong

Violence as air
Malicious mockery
started a guilty thing

Trumpet shrill-sounding
Sea or fire/ earth or air
extravagant and erring

confine this sent object
Wholesome power
gracious time

walk our watch tonight
Loves let's celebrate dawn
all night long

You're Mine You

A person of many solitudes
they give valediction
they give from instinct infinitesimal selves
they keep pained expressions out of the household
they disregard infinitesimal selves

Unceasingly they aren't public
unending under unending another not subconsciously
They aren't alike parallel to some center
They aren't unalike from some surface equality

They stay

They unberth haters w/ difficulty
They wake apart/ untethered/ boundless
They forget waking apart and then they begin
They make w/ infinitesimal selves

They aren't stable tethered
They aren't wild apart
They are revealed
They yes longer possessionless

Equanimity became a nest
they created

Pressed Against This Smart Glass

Happen to find yourself a particular afternoon notice a makeshift craft
floating through the narrow and bounded by steep shoulders waterway

Notice fairies harnessed/ boiled a ramshackle armada of miracles
from the comparative wilderness
caught that afternoon
Care evidently distrusting the order 'wanted alive'

Hollowed out logs lashed to a skinny man w/ a burlap sack deemed to be snoozing
A rent in the net under the weight of streams blanketed with moss

The sun already knows my nickname
An arrow shot clean through my ribs
Clock fragmented clots of day
plan/ plant/ drain the fertile forest hills

The wilderness riding me out across out-of-print autobiography
w/ a resonance of mathematics learned bargaining sharply
for apples can tease murderers and settlers to domesticate the frontier with old world exotics

Disparagement might return a golden habitat
an emblem of marriage
from man's peculiar craft

passengers point at a sign
Working for food
Waiting for the bumblebee to wake up to hover among wide-eyed

We give credit the power domestication represents
take to dance
Generations assume naive scenes

Animals sit it out
Nutritious acorns buried any arrangement with us long before
boatloads dependent on bank territory or at least the folk hero I figured

Modest our orchard or/
our childlike wishful/ wistful thinking
how lost

We accept fate in the tang of strangeness sweetened beyond recognition
a blemish-free plastic dimension
one all-purpose-single-use-just-as-described-cheap-fake-sugar-substitute for the strong desire to live to

lounge in queerness
with no address
Hallow defiance

a night swim
a vegan frontier
do you mind
to ride a horse or punish a worm

Children are not rumors

For some cis-godfearing-rapist-white-men emphasis relies on her dress/ color of skin/

mitigation/ migration/ maps

Some far-flung account/ song led to the river
the reality and the pipe littered behind

Ololyga

Evocation

Crest shoulder
wing
breast holder
ring
dress folder
sing
rest holder
cling
clean
organize
bring
scream
dream
steam
seam
stream

lean
rest holder
lean

Opal

under heft
falling
crest-down
lunging
sour left pocket
knuckle meat
wrench
soul trunk
back hand
food

Lesson

swollen over
less called on
left food
a weight
some water
down eyes
lark step
need-hold

bawling
stripped muscle
slipped wrangle
smart watch
right angle
striped food
stippled

Irony

Food for mules
left breast
right hand pocket
tone down or plead
want now/ or need
hand down or bleed
earnest seed
launch now for food
breast buckle
meet hook
love knot
vacuum trout
drought face

Hope

Last pattern of a lock
last goods
too late to tread
fear too close
to good
to holdless good
to oldness-hood
kindness food
unveil heart
sped thread hustle
fodder

Love knot

One lock
sex and peace
hold to bone
one love stance
electric ache

over strain
another warm bone frame
lone stone in wonder
one fire
here

Hold tight then

lost to shackling
lost to shocking
conformation

Coupling

live bit
suppression
explosion
love bites
live bit
young-love
anger-love
self-love
love

who cannot walk among these
who will find them

Public fear

Crooked contagion
another leader lost
another woman defamed
people gone
of denigration
countries gone
viral with hate
viral with virus
cities shelter in place
nurses gone
restaurants/ workers gone
postal/ grocery workers
migrant workers gone
farmers/ gardeners
loved ones
disappeared

Families despair

families born
of fear

families born
w/ love

families born
repair

Prayer

Left corpuscle
warm crease
leaden heart
water bowl
of light

Beginning an End

Everyone is indoors for weeks as we seek
the nowhere everyone went to
summer's either-all highways
Remember community secrets
papyri stay

The chill either memorized shoulder blades
or we bought our ego-other's obstruction
Said no last bold point
Bold, possessing emptiness
Where we seek substance

only closed space
light sealed solid against boulders/
caliche/ cacti No ticking day No void
Only us finite things

sober/ alone Reason
made tight made no stillness
Our skin is sighted
only no one stopped by
to pick us up

Papas/ Dead on the Ground

All of those newly minted ancient wet realms
Dream figures like natures desire practitioners
Plants equally drive marrying power
Artificial selection— Darwins ever

expanding All of them in the garden
hardworking in lab coats monster-drug-grower-
financiers fanatical about trucks lifting a basket
This sweet wreck standing— that's wildness

To make us daughters gardeners press every
angle/ chapter/ gene deem the parse answer
proposing unexpected multifarious lives Leave us
exactly everything surrounding seeds/

microbes/ animals/ effulgence teaming
any literal sense not a white wilderness
with the cherished perilous grace to embrace
the garden fence with staggering geometry

to believe the gardener knows the opposite
of garden probably because yes well less wild
the world and tensions rose Declension/
malevolence of daunting spurts my basket-full

on our domestic threshold the moment the harvest
ransacked can't very well maraud to stand raw
flesh blankly welcoming a hint of comfort
at least the smell of the Earth called mint

as great a blessing as needed to be dug
left in the ground dead on looking for abandonment to
a tear bottled as if distilled soil
Fresh spring fresh earthy earthly feeling most

giving spade that moist fingers incarnate
Undifferentiated fires— sunny satanic
translucent faceted forms like any genetic
instruction adjacent rocks determine shape

a symmetry of seeds adds potatoes alike those known
to a fit happier always given somehow heavier
always cooler stone Because the eye/ the hand

the implement/ identity the unmistakable basket

around feelings feeling around inured fingers you're forcing
to download go for the bruise app to ease your aside
Play the *or else what* first flash gathering the fresh
taupe earth/ cloth/ clods/ the velvet crust the spade turns

My Scapegoat Wound

The decision head long ago
really didn't matter
the question's status quo

to drug our confidence
with exactly what governance
called the point

It almost seemed new
w/ the sort of idea of cooking
the skin buttered through

looked and tasted well
as luscious flesh
fingerlings around toes

August leaves eating
off pudding probably pepper bellies
bags of McDonald's plenty

I've eaten my hands
biotech or not—
my cropped harvest

wish wound wound new
leaves betwixt loppers
a scapegoat insect incision

to clone/ check
a gorgeous looking slice of home
after August

This You an Echo November Abandons

A shallow brace set under the pile-driven epoch crumbling on its subject

You don't have it all
from keeping your mouth shut

You from lips me?

Nothing is the largest snap
No one lawless bound me too

We have
nothing unbound

Won't I sit
unbending/ unbeing/ unsexing/
lawless/ silent

No way
never
I'll win
every mind

My sour heart?
Empowerment

held drunk within your freedom

Our people
aren't the same
nor you

Nor you
Nothing is this stayed within me
In none indignant sea

Under Trees

Her piano quickens me
w/ its great glass garbage
it's a reverie in all green

as the shallowest edge of the river
reflects the canopy clear through
to the reach of the sky

To fear nighttime
is no apostrophe

Monitors beam
marriage as the image of purgatory
homicide as the turning point
of love and desire
Gods fight over who is the god

Or god is breath
aspirating death

Sources

Listed by chapter the principle facts are influenced by human bumblebee David's life whose probably more than any other open-eyes nature

with the point of view of plants-imagination-rooted-in-fact *what amorous amounts of books* particularly illuminating a classic agriculture of people wild animals cultivate/ culture/

choose domestication conservation Environmental winter essays by the fire bring into context what constitutes fitness during the Neolithic era, then guns, germs and the fates

Disarm fake history hand botany the long quadrant of Manhattan an excellent precipitant some do not apprise the women's journey in science and math manages to rise

Of angiosperms during the native seed's search American agriculture *point* press-on evolution selects the origin of the selfish press Perilous grace— the meanings of life

how the leopard's spots ghost the origin house for the red queen penguin city of night
To the diversity of the University of the Diversity of Diverse Life

About the Hype

I want to write more so probably won't Mad Mad myth
Here is a portrait of the hero I was to hope for

whose source of life remains math this smith match
Her stoical figure showing me a debt

to excellence Pro indigenous and immigrant heritage
biographical hearts desire historically brutal books

The Wilderness Anthology of American Anatomy
An Apple-sourced experiment books on "wink" modern fruit science/

ecological imperialism/ the press/ special round pills We all
profit from conversations with the OCD (orchard conservation department)

Also reading our obituary as myth and old news
of seeds carried by canoe with an orchardist and journalist visiting the big apple

An Oh Well Star

Baste me with salve
blast me into a gush of honey
wake me before my bones become hollow

Subject to hate bring on fever
I wallow/ sweat/ swallow
in sheets of mud

Screech a pitch to shatter the stars/
the gods Shards of cracked earth tumble
down a crest Lightning sinters my chest

A later day lover feels the welt before my heart

How can I feed a swell of hands over sand
rolling into a bawl

My fevered bleat
to breach your guise
synesthesia/ my garments/ lungs
billow as a sail forced to the wind road

I find myself set against self
twined to error bidding me to air
bellows through us
a pregnant platter of torn flesh

Bones rattle the wind
Bottles of glass scatter
and shatter through the wash
scoring white hot

Scalloped I reach for a length of rhyme
to tie around fingers to remind
two reminders with a bow to be kind

Too weak to self-soothe
another creature without legs
cracks a welt along my cheekbone

an oh well star burning in the wind for poems

Mineral tock of a stalagmite/
pendulum/ podium/ drop

to a frenzy of nonchalance
Just grab that mossy wedge

The derangement of tenderness

I make way with the rate of my cranium
for berries

Manacled priests and joyous children
wander about the path I tend

Times incise
Sharks crave the deep

Challenge eleven sills before the force of the flood
Swollen fleet of ministers hazardous from hell

don't fear yourself
the silken shadow of birth
your mothers' breath

Ololyga breaks
from the outskirts to the square

We'll fine/
refine the subject
chain/ break the true fake

cast aside that foolhardy pulpiteer
to a cacophony of coyotes wild over one rat

Sirens come rushing a thug president
tethered to the front gates as one tweet as numbly
as a gale through fenestration bursts his yellow heart

One split fatty seed stills us to the cheek of an empty belly
Hunger cuts the sweet violence of a pot of gold

His letter had arrived with pros and coins to little fanfare
Dis was a god once rapist god seeking her out of heaven

sweltering she humidifies heat
swell in such climates

Room cons womb

Rare sorrow from such spleen food
Yellow as urine chicken broth

fighter and feather
pillow of wonder

As fuel breaches a fire fence
we leap from climate dreams

Arrange a highlight where we sleep
The coyotes howl their watch along the sand

See the sea rise and sea foam shed from a rock
Form a welcoming

Interview the demagogues
How many cataracts will seep into a drizzle

before the flood waters rise
Our retribution patents cries

Crack each staff
with alternative facts

From sunlit parched lips
skull dead skin and eyes

try not to try

Little one/ what love

It's a *good* thing I'm no Van Gogh
Here for an hour
here unhinged

some neighbor's friend
fresh can snap
dust burst

stark
yellow
hollow

orphan day snaked
through cornsilk
coiled in corn flour

we spin us
in the dust devil of
spirits we love

we how old we
and ankle yet
an hour's till hours still
ours our ours

The feeling second I inhale
vapor I want to embrace her
get right to her hummingbird zoom

our hearts catching take plunder
there's no time to wrench
freedom from fear

quake with our liberty
with this world ache

we'll embrace here

I know I know it's hard for the hive
the drive to thrive the vibe too anxious
to practice keys or strum guitar
my education wasn't
wasted on me

how cold
what times
a spider

inches at a cat
saunters we are
wonders winter's/
Walter's daughters
on a crag spinning to
stop over We can't turn
some frozen night back
we can only be like this
midnight mild bi-pedal stargazing along

You know you know how
our mortal earth splayed
the early-morning-all-day-

late-night-centuries with a lathe
arteries cartography injected
die spinning

stopping in oblivion
like any living being
or inventing and deciphering to fast

for a radical proof to cure the night
with hesitation we *all perish*
we're all some thing

the brim of a generation
conceived and bred we make our
damned world *Now*

have some stew
try again with this
roof toil wasp's nest

A world too and quiet
this link scanning across my wow

what magic humanity
has to sing to carry

to cry following gravity
drips upon my lip

a leaf of pigment from my frail
quill not a grid or heavy heart

stolen lighter forgotten visage
shards or fibers from a girl

her reflection or hair void of this
whirl

How lucky to live
to hear a donkey bray

in proximity the word settles
on a census or some

war-torn echoing evil refrain
rape used as a weapon in Ukraine

mirroring refraction rarefacting
this nesting dove screeching away

If haft hast if heft
a swallow floats down
with love for this fig bush

I help grow for the world
pulmonary rush
exhale to make art

a hollow stalk
to blow across
or through bamboo

hot wind and music
desert oasis shake
laugh hello golden wasp

at rest in the breeze
a mellow moment
bling of ease

bells swing
swell this still point
what wonders turning cease

to weep under the stream
of negligence to be free

What do these bones want to say

snarl a jokeless rasp insect instant
stroke of quiet stokes the west
wind fuels my fear for water

the last hollow well we'll fill
with regular strangled Moan

restart the motor
You well you rifle our life sit
back adjust your tie

defame any other for *exactly* what it is you are up to
People died
for your lies

To Rio so as like
to dance

masked so as not
to die

yet stay in
to kill

this virus
fear in place

here safe
this croaking

lizard
mouse rustling

rabbit
I am an idiot

a pulsing heart
We swell

make away stay inside
celebrate

our two faces
face to face

About the Type

Digital technology and dexterity
of a highly beautiful renaissance type
combine fonts (primarily hype)
the readable non-fungible kind

face classical inspired by design or
golden originals pressed in a book
paint ecological imperialism as our last
kiss modular-fruit-science centers

diversity visiting the orchardist
now journalist borrowing New York
apples of helpful environmental history
on Apple's books and wink

an apple-sourced experiment from which
orchard conversations supplanted profit
for the common good Old and a mess
our obituaries become an anthology

of historical wilderness " *This*
is American Idol" our contemporary idiom
and read poetry Our heart's desire printed
in intersectional feminist texts a debt too true

to figures showing me health
indispensable en masse
between botany insta and news
samsara and hope for me and you

Rub a Raw Slice Down the Middle or Modern Plants

My porch the limbo back when young leaves botched the ordinary harvest to garden the modified genetic why perfect the flame under blown out and understood suddenly to opt for the choice given a big bowl of home no doubt to tell them all of course we're counting

on neighbors with Cheerios *will ask* made me smile well ask gave me fear Perfectly safe at the picnic though this obvious chance of water supper a beach invitation still the fireworks splay the way we work the middle slice up a raw cleave sticking keeping me that is

methodically untouched Thanking vacation the porch remained New leaves summer weeks late *would you want let me ask Was there* I press before a destination to select before a hint of the effect a new kiss gleans the same not simply

strong phenomenon of substantial equivalence that the asterisk pointed to as safe proof we could offer critique of a molecular avarice with tests/ scientists a safe potato has one machine metaphor bugs with evidently *to kill to eat together*

at The Best Bureaucratic-Pestilence-Wonderland a bit like the jurisdiction of eyes least/ lash/ regard Turned out freedom always assumed safety has been voluntary when the regulation /religion /surgeon of modified facts operates on me

Valediction Forbidding Treason

I hear a shoal of shells crush under leather feel thick hairy calves of impenetrable women lift the rope *ho* the enormous hate strangled in sargassum at the shore everybody helps hilarious fruitful ideas shudder and quicken against the net a great snap blisters our hands heaving the sea we burn the carcass clean
we dance
birds pester
insects crack

One stalks one lonely one desperate to speak we need to be among each other to listen for some anapest ache close at hand take my flesh to beach another breath to breach another swell I will find you I will take your face into my hands I will kiss your forehead and
your lips
I'm steady
take sway

Loose your footing she swells we make each other's way all womaned down to the end of the hard times and to the joyous flatter us play my heart chugs/ speeds up we are made of our mothers' breath we are her shadow and her ground we are well and jumbled like kids drunk in the dance spinning/ skidding/ prancing to the side/ jumping columns/ capitals crowned with acanthus shading four eyes crumble a militarized capitalist stroll to the chapel we run shouting/ chanting violence virus
the citadel is breached
unidentified police
screeching violins

Taking the Lady's Hand and Passing Her Back Her Bag

"Do you know how I know that I love you

[the breath egressing from her left nostril
echoes off her eardrum and sounds like wind]

earlier today I thought how I would be if you died"

That's love, the death fantasy, our enumeration of loss The rescue fantasy signifies fornication or the desire to save to be deep-ended upon

"be if you died"

Come rushing the assailant faster than a sound can pass from the mouth of your dear victim No, you catch the victim as she falls You hold her to your chest as you rest her with the strength of your left arm on the sidewalk You leap for the assailant hug him around the ankles send him smashing to the cement kneel into his back your arm around his neck

if you died now today

Why does the rescue fantasy come when you want to get sexual and the death fantasy come with love? The rescue fantasy is thrilling and not often followed by the depth fanta [sigh]

Remember what it's like?

"do you know how I know that I love you
because earlier today I thought how I would
be if you died
be
if you died now today"

Raising her hand here

More

Motopoiesis breaks
shards
[chatter
 ]

Transparent Kitchen

I bite each seashell gem between my teeth
to remind us we have bodies to please
each other with *Translucent buttons pop*
I lied about you not having my heart
Through a veil of beads I'm bound to your sleeve

Have it my love to mend each seam and hem
Minds /limbs/ our desire unjumbled then
on the kitchen floor Our tender buttons
among shorn garlands, scissors, ash and bone
"I have just now vacuumed," I lied That kiss
the first upon our lips always just now

We sound the word poem as elision Poem
as half a foot We speak in poems like we
dream up our lucky columbarium

Little One/ What Love

Fire flowers to the west Flames father
a mother cardinal's gyre switching swirl
Malevolent rhetorical world made
to twist sense systems sanctimonious
primordial provider violence

Delusions allude to the opposite
to apostate Do your dear Earth help See
we need our cure *are* equanimity
our primer one sweetest blossom of fuel
waiting for a hummingbird to sync *Wait*

for her to alight two eggs as like as
mint Tic Tacs in a downy nest of webs
or a baby tar ball on lizard legs
to *wait only* perch with alert darling

Left Hand It the World Rolling

The roar of waves curling towards the soft shore I diving off a cliff refract
the cosign might of the harvest moon dress four early morn the grinding stone/
flour/ coffee beans/ steam/ chatter/ rolling/ along track across a field razing
reaping buying land growing hot houseplants planting roots my teeth ache anger
and ink in sleep each sweet-swell-sea-shell-crown-chakra-super-moon-charged-
crystal-oil *love it* Watch this calm catch the light high and tight glint of palm Pollen
pitched to the sky a hummingbird alights before a searing last ray of *lethal aid* I
squander/ ignite one death-cult-capitalist-lite-acid-calm night

Ecologue

What are this chaste
the in-charge rose
freshly longer stem
short green thorns
over potato vines
the squashy shade
slugs happy as lettuces
dug lamps in big leaves
staked in earth a cane
trellis the trailed pumpkin
yellow pods and green
bulging sunflowers
the tops of beans
paths and arteries
that's my geometry
to burst the threatening fruit ripe
rampant anarchy of summertime
the end of always week's end
a couple in the garden

My deep gratitude to the following presses, publications, and organizations:

Cathexis Northwest Press
Finishing Line Press
Damaged Goods Press
Genre: Urban Arts
Querencia
Sundress Publications
Beyond Queer Words
Global Poemic
High Shelf Press
The Night Heron Barks
Not Your Mother's Breast Milk
Ran Off with the Star Bassoon
Saint Mary's Magazine
Sunspot Literary Journal
Tulane Review
Wild Roof Journal

C. M. Tollefson, Mirto Stone, Laurie Saurborn, Drew Krewer, Susan Briante, Farid Matuk, T.C. Tolbert, Sara Sams, C. A. Conrad and Susan Nguyen, thank you, always just now.

Notes on the text:

I selected the initial lexicon for "To Lovers Who Canoe the Day," "Deities and the Human Brain," "City's Limit," "About the Type," "About the Hype," "*Papas*/ Dead on the Ground," "Sources," "My Scapegoat Wound," "Frailer Neighbors," "Pressed Against this Smart Glass," "Rub a Raw Slice Down the Middle or Modern Plants," and "Ecologue" from Michael Pollan's *The Botany of Desire*. In most cases I chose up to three consecutive words from a page or pages of Pollan's prose. For a few poems I selected the text in reverse. Four of the poems are derived from the back matter. I dictated the selected text to my phone. Voice recognition added some surprising turns when it misheard. Initially favoring sound over sense, I rearranged the block of recorded text. Meaning, vocabulary, cuts, line breaks, stanzas, and transpositions followed.

"Dress Our Souls" was an opposite emulation of Robert Duncan's "The Song of the Borderguard." I chose an opposite or opposites for each word in his poem as the first draft of my poem.

"Petal" is an erasure from Act.1 Scene. 1 of William Shakespeare's *Hamlet*.

My title "You're Mine You" is Chet Baker's song title. The poem began as an opposite emulation of a love letter from my wife.

Ololyga in ancient Greece was "a ritual shout peculiar to females." See Anne Carson's essay, "The Gender of Sound."

"Beginning an End" was an opposite emulation of Pablo Neruda's "Poetry."

"This You an Echo November Abandons" was an opposite emulation of Emily Dickinson's [I've none to tell me to but Thee].

I sing parts of "Taking the Lady's Hand and Passing Her Back Her Bag."

"An Oh Well Star" is a three-part poem in progress.

From "Transparent Kitchen" the phrase "tender buttons" is an allusion to Gertrude Stein's *Tender Buttons.*

"Valediction Forbidding Treason" alludes to John Donne's "A Valediction Forbidding Mourning."

Valyntina is a multi-genre eco artist living with her wife in Tucson, Arizona. She works with paint, ink, Neon, encaustic medium, recycled or repurposed materials and words. She is the author of three poetry chapbooks, the tête-bêche *Fever Dream/ Take Heart* (Cathexis Northwest Press 2020) and *In Our Now* (Finishing Line Press 2022). Find more of her work at valyntinagrenier.com or find her on Insta @valyntinagrenier.

Also Available from Cathexis Northwest Press:

Something To Cry About
by Robert Krantz

Suburban Hermeneutics
by Ian Cappelli

God's Love Is Very Busy
by David Seung

that one time we were almost people
by Christian Czaniecki

Fever Dream/Take Heart
by Valyntina Grenier

The Book of Night & Waking
by Clif Mason

Dead Birds of New Zealand
by Christian Czaniecki

The Weathering of Igneous Rockforms in High-Altitude Riparian Environments
by John Belk

If A Fish
by George Burns

How to Draw a Blank
by Collin Van Son

En Route
by Jesse Wolfe

sky bright psalms
by Temple Cone

Moonbird
by Henry G. Stanton

southern athiest. oh, honey
by d. e. fulford

Bruises, Birthmarks & Other Calamities
by Nadine Klassen

Wanted: Comedy, Addicts
by AR Dugan

They Curve Like Snakes
by David Alexander McFarland

the catalog of daily fears
by Beth Dufford

Shops Close Too Early
by Josh Feit

Vanity Unfair and Other Poems
by Robert Eugene Rubino

Destructive Heresies
by Milo E. Gorgevska

Bodies of Separation
by Chim Sher Ting

The Night with James Dean and Other Prose Poems
by Allison A. deFreese

About Time
by Julie Benesh

Suspended
by Ellen White Rook

The Unempty Spaces Between
by Louis Efron

Quomodo probatur in conflatorio
by Nick Roberts

Call Me Not Ishmael but the Sea
by J. Martin Daughtry

Wild Evolution
by Naomi Leimsider

Acta
by Patrick Wilcox

Practising Ascending
by Nadine Hitchiner

Cathexis Northwest Press

www.ingramcontent.com/pod-product-compliance
Lightning Source LLC
Chambersburg PA
CBHW030351100526
44592CB00010B/907
* 9 7 8 1 9 5 2 8 6 9 8 4 6 *